The Mysterious  & Unknown

Ghosts

by Gail B. Stewart

ReferencePoint Press™

San Diego, CA

For more information, contact:
ReferencePoint Press, Inc.
PO Box 27779
San Diego, CA 92198
www.ReferencePointPress.com

Picture credits:
Cover: Istockphoto
AP Images: 24, 26, 27, 29, 34, 41, 44, 45, 71, 80, 85, 93
Dreamstime: 48
Istockphoto: 51
North Wind: 13, 16, 19, 22
Science Photo Library: 8, 11, 59

Series design and book layout:
Amy Stirnkorb

LIBRARY OF CONGRESS CATALOGING-IN-PUBLICATION DATA

Stewart, Gail B.
Ghosts / Gail B. Stewart.
  p. cm. -- (Mysterious & unknown series)
  Includes bibliographical references and index.

ISBN-13: 978-1-60152-032-6 (hardback)
ISBN-10: 1-60152-032-8 (hardback)
1. Ghosts. I. Title.
BF1461.P37 2008

133.1--dc22   2007032267

CONTENTS

FOREWORD

"Strange is our situation here upon earth."
—*Albert Einstein*

Since the beginning of recorded history, people have been
perplexed, fascinated, and even terrified by events that defy
explanation. While science has demystified many of these events,
such as volcanic eruptions and lunar eclipses, some remain outside
the scope of the provable. Do UFOs exist? Are people abducted by
aliens? Can some people see into the future? These questions and
many more continue to puzzle, intrigue, and confound despite the
enormous advances of modern science and technology.

It is these questions, phenomena, and oddities that Reference-
Point Press's *The Mysterious & Unknown* series is committed to
exploring. Each volume examines historical and anecdotal evidence
as well as the most recent theories surrounding the topic in debate.
Fascinating primary source quotes from scientists, experts, and
eyewitnesses as well as in-depth sidebars further inform the text.
Full-color illustrations and photos add to each book's visual appeal.
Finally, source notes, a bibliography, and a thorough index provide
further reference and research support. Whether for research or
the curious reader, *The Mysterious & Unknown* series is certain to
satisfy those fascinated by the unexplained.

INTRODUCTION

The Ghosts in the Attic

The first time Mark Houser heard the voices, he was annoyed. The 42-year-old divorced father of two had come home from work a little early and heard voices upstairs on the third floor. At first he thought his two children were skipping school. But as he listened more carefully, he realized both voices were those of small children—far younger than his own two teenagers. As he walked upstairs to investigate, the voices suddenly stopped. Thinking he must have heard noises from outside, he went back downstairs and did not give the episode another thought.

A few nights later, however, he awoke and heard the same voices again. He recalls lying in bed wondering if he was imagining them. He considered that it could be intruders and debated whether he should get up and look. He remembers thinking, "Am I crazy? Do I run upstairs and confront them? Or do

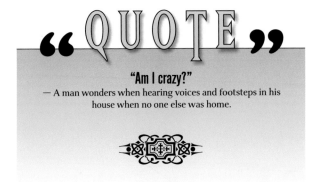

I bolt out the door?"[1] He decided to head upstairs, but again, just as he reached the top of the stairs, the voices stopped. Later, he admitted that he decided not to investigate. "It really scared me," he says. "I went back to bed and literally pulled the covers over my head. There was something in my house, and I really was too frightened to think about it in the middle of the night."[2]

"I Didn't Think You'd Believe Me"

Houser wondered about his own sanity. He was not prone to an overactive imagination, and these voices worried him. "I didn't know what was happening," Houser says. "I wondered if I was cracking up, if maybe the stress of the divorce was finally hitting me."[3] But he was stunned a few days later when he drove to his ex-wife's home to pick up his children for the weekend. She told him that neither his 15-year-old son nor his 13-year-old daughter wanted to come to his house. The reason, she informed Houser, was ghosts.

Both teens had heard the voices when they were at his house. But his son actually *saw* the ghosts the last time he was there. Houser's reaction was a mixture of terror and relief, he recalls. "I was scared, of course," he says, "because of what my son had seen but relieved that I wasn't crazy. What I heard must be what he had seen. I asked him why he hadn't told me when it happened, and he said, 'I didn't think you'd believe me.'"[4]

Houser was baffled. His son seemed certain that he had seen

the ghost of a boy bouncing a ball upstairs. He had also heard the voices several times while staying at his father's house. But though Houser considered himself open-minded about most things, the idea of ghosts was absurd. "Any supernatural explanation was too farfetched," he says. "I didn't believe in that stuff."[5]

Getting Help

Over the next several days, however, Houser realized that other odd things were going on in the house. In the basement, for instance, he bumped into something solid but invisible. He encountered an unexplainable cold spot in the living room near the piano. And there was the frequent sound of someone bouncing a basketball up on the third floor in the middle of the night.

Houser had never believed in spirits or ghosts. He was sure that there had to be some reasonable explanation. But when it was evident that the noises were not being made by squirrels, a malfunctioning furnace, water pipes, or intruders, he decided to try something different. He called in a psychic, who told him that he had not one but four ghosts in his house. He would have no peace, she informed him, until they left.

"I Don't Dial Astrology 1-800"

Houser could not see the ghosts, nor could he hear their responses to the questions the psychic was asking them. However, he was willing to participate when she told him it would be best if he helped her tell the ghosts to leave. Ghosts, she explained, are the spirits of people who have died. These spirits are supposed to leave Earth and pass on into the afterlife, often referred to as "the other side." However, in some cases they are unable or unwilling to do so. By insisting that these spirits must leave the house and

Ghosts are the spirits of people who have died. These spirits are supposed to leave Earth and pass on into the afterlife, often referred to as "the other side." However, in some cases they are unable or unwilling to do so.

pass on into the afterlife, Houser and the psychic were able to rid the house of ghosts.

Houser had never believed in ghosts before. Even today, he is not sure he completely understands what occurred in his house. He admits that before this happened, he would have been very skeptical of any story about ghost children bouncing balls in someone's home. He says he is not the kind of person who is quick to believe in such things.

"I wondered why this happened to me," Houser says. "I've done pretty well financially because I'm a good communicator and I'm not an extremist. I don't dial Astrology 1-800. I don't drink, I don't use drugs. I'm a health nut. I don't eat sugar. I've run seven or eight marathons. What I'm trying to say is I'm a conservative guy. I don't feel the need for people to believe me on this. But there it is."[6]

"You Just Can't Close That Door"

Houser is one of many who have had experiences with ghosts or spirits. And like many of those, he is sure that few people will believe him. Interestingly, however, statistics seem to indicate otherwise. For example, a 2005 CBS poll found that 48 percent of Americans say they believe ghosts exist, and one in five has personally seen or felt the presence of a ghost.

"You just can't dismiss it," says Julius, who also experienced what appeared to be ghost activity in his Indiana home. "Even though it seems too weird. You just can't close that door. I mean, who knows what's on the other side, right?"[7]

Did You Know?

Ghosts are purported to be spirits of people who have died.

CHAPTER 1

A World of Spirits

History is filled with stories of people who have seen or felt the presence of ghosts. Thousands of stories and legends tell of encounters with the spirit world, some dating back centuries. How many of these stories are true is unknown, but many researchers suspect that many are at least grounded in real events.

Death and the Spirit

The idea of ghosts is based on how a particular culture views death. Most religions teach that a human being is not only a physical body but also a spirit or soul that lives on after the physical body dies. Some religions teach that this soul immediately leaves the body after death and goes to a spirit world such as heaven where it will live eternally. Other religions, such as Buddhism, believe that souls go temporarily to a spirit world while they await rebirth, or reincarnation.

Plato, the famous Greek philosopher, warned in his dialogue Phaedo *that it can be dangerous for people to spend any time around tombs and graveyards as they may encounter ghosts.*

Did You Know?

The idea of ghosts is based on how a particular culture views death.

A ghost is usually defined as a spirit or soul that is earthbound for some reason. Such a spirit has chosen not to move to its spirit world or is somehow unable to make the transition. In those instances, the spirit lingers among the living, occasionally making its presence known.

One of the first written references to such earthbound spirits came from the fourth century B.C. philosopher Plato. In his dialogue *Phaedo* he warned how dangerous it was for people "prowling about tombs and sepulchers, near which, as they tell us, are seen certain ghostly apparitions of souls which have not departed pure."[8]

The First Written Ghost Story

Though stories of the terror caused by ghosts have been around for thousands of years, a letter from the 1st century A.D. might be the first written account of a house haunted by ghosts. The letter, written by the Roman teacher Pliny the Younger, describes a beautiful estate in Athens that no one would dare rent because it was rumored to have a ghost.

> The folk told how at the end of night horrid noises were heard: the clanking of chains which grew louder and louder until there suddenly appeared the hideous phantom of an old man who seemed the very picture of abject filth and misery. His beard was long and matted, his white hair disheveled and unkempt. His thin legs were loaded with a weight of galling [chains] that he dragged wearily along with a painful moaning.

In Ireland generations ago, the cry of the banshee was an unwelcome noise. It was believed that the banshee, the ghost of a beautiful woman, could foretell a death.

Pliny goes on to explain that many people doubted the ghost's existence, but it did not take long for them to be convinced otherwise: "Some mocking skeptics who were once bold enough to watch all night in the house had been well-nigh scared from their senses at the sight of the apparition. . . . A placard 'To Let' was posted, but year succeeded year and the house fell almost to ruin and decay."[9]

One man—a philosopher named Athenodorus who was very short of money—was not terribly worried about the ghost. He needed a place to live and gladly paid the low price asked by the renter. The first night in his new home, he was visited by the ghost, who motioned for Athenodorus to follow him outside. Frightened, the man refused, but when the ghost proceeded to rattle his chains, he agreed and followed the spirit into the garden. The ghost did not remain long—it pointed at a patch of ground and vanished.

Athenodorus told his story to the authorities the next day, and they dug up the garden. There they found human remains that were still bound in heavy chains. The bones were then buried according to custom, and the ghost never returned. Evidently, Pliny wrote, the ghost had been uneasy because it had not had a proper burial.

Spirits Everywhere

Ghosts and spirits have been a part of almost every culture throughout the world. The Shinto religion, practiced since ancient times in Japan, teaches about a netherworld—a midway point between death and eternal life in the spirit world. While in this netherworld, angry or frustrated ghosts, called *kami*, can return to Earth and cause problems for the living.

In Ireland generations ago, the cry of the banshee was an unwelcome noise. It was believed that the banshee, the ghost of a beautiful woman, could foretell a death. People who heard the echoing wail of the banshee, as she walked under the moon in her long green dress, knew that a friend or loved one would likely be dead by morning.

Generations ago in Russia and other Slavic nations, people believed in spirits called *domovoi*, the ghosts of male ancestors that returned to Earth to watch over their families. Each *domovik*—usually the ghost of a deceased grandfather or great-grandfather—lived behind the family stove. Although *domovoi* were believed to be helpful, they were also demanding. It was crucially important to please the *domovik* by putting out food for it or consulting it on important decisions. If the family's *domovik* were ignored or forgotten, the spirit could make trouble. Angry *domovoi* were known to make loud noises at night to scare their families, or in some extreme instances they would even burn their houses down. If a family moved, they took a few coals from the stove to make certain their *domovik* followed them to their new home.

Modern Ghosts

Through the centuries people have shared a sometimes uneasy relationship with the spirit world. Castles in Europe have been inhabited by generations of ghosts. Tales are told of haunted battlegrounds, ships piloted by ghostly crews, and angry spirits of murder victims demanding revenge among the living.

And while fewer cultures today practice daily rituals to appease spirits, as they once did, the spirits are still not forgotten. Mexico is one of several countries that celebrate a day of the

A ghost ship piloted by a spirit crew lures another ship to its doom in the rocky waters off a coastline.

dead to honor spirits of family and friends with parties, food, and the tidying of graves. It is believed that if the spirits are happy, they will not return to Earth. Halloween, too, began as a night when children dressed up as the ghosts believed to be roaming Earth every October 31.

For most people today ghosts are simply the stuff of legends and scary movies, but many others believe that ghosts actually do exist. Among the believers are psychics and mediums who say that they can communicate with spirits. Others are ghost investigators, who hope that by using a range of scientific tools they can gather data that can scientifically prove the existence of ghosts. And finally, some are people who have had experiences that they cannot explain and can only attribute to ghosts.

Foolish Fire

Ghost investigators say that ghosts make themselves known to the living in a number of ways. Some appear as a light or a group of lights—which is a mystery all its own since no logical source for such light can be found. It is often referred to as *ignis fatuus*, a Latin phrase meaning "foolish fire"—so called because one would be foolish to attempt to catch or capture it.

This light has been seen on ancient Roman battlefields and sites of roadside bombings in the Middle East. It has been spotted in cemeteries and farm fields. People have reported seeing it in windows of unoccupied houses and hovering over the scenes of long-ago murders.

Ghost investigator Janis Raley says that unexplained lights such as these have various shapes and sizes. "We have seen some that look like small bubbles, cinnamon buns, and a bad cases of the hives," she says. "They can occur as single orbs, in clusters, in whirling clumps, be bright as stars, or be barely visible. They can look radically different, but are recognizable as the same general type of phenomena."[10]

A Face on a Billboard

Another way for a ghost to appear is by means of a two-dimensional image. It might be a hazy likeness of a dead person that appears on a wall or even suspended in midair. The image does not speak or attempt to communicate, say researchers.

One such image appeared in the summer of 1991 after the brutal murder of a little girl in Chula Vista, California. The victim, nine-year-old Laura Arroyo, was kidnapped from her home after she ran to answer the doorbell. A moment after she ran to the door, her mother went to see who had arrived, but there was no sign of anyone—including Laura. Sixteen hours later, however, her battered body was found several miles from her home.

People expressed outrage and concern that something so terrible could happen in their community. And then, just a few days after the murder, a strange thing happened. An image of a little girl's face appeared on an empty billboard about two miles from the murder scene. People were aghast, for the face looked like that of Laura.

"What Is She Trying to Say?"

Word of the ghostly image spread throughout Chula Vista and nearby San Diego. Over the next few weeks huge crowds—between 20,000 and 30,000 each night—arrived just before sunset. As the skies darkened, the ghostly image of the girl's face appeared. Even those who had been skeptical before were astonished by what they saw. "I heard about this from friends,"

In Ireland,
the cry of the
banshee was an
unwelcome noise.
It was believed that
the banshee, the
ghost of a beautiful
woman, could
foretell a
death.

One way that ghosts can make themselves known is in a mirror.
Abraham Lincoln saw a double image of himself in the mirror shortly
before he was elected president in 1860. One image was his normal
self, but the second image was a clearly ill Lincoln—almost deathlike.
Lincoln believed that it was a premonition. The unhealthy appearance of the second image, he believed, meant he would die during his
second term in office. He was shot and killed in April 1865.

one teacher said, "but until now I didn't believe it. Her face is definitely there."[11]

A Chula Vista police officer, sent to the scene because of the huge traffic jams, came back to the station shaken by what he had seen. He reported that he, too, was sure that it was Laura's face. "We were all surprised when he came back with this report,"[12] admitted his senior officer, Lieutenant Merlin Wilson.

Many believed the image was the spirit of Laura, perhaps returning to Earth to ask that her murderer be found. "There is an energy in the world we don't know about," said one witness. "I believe in the supernatural. Whether or not this is it, I don't know. But it's just too strange, when you can look up and see too clearly her mouth and eyes. It makes me wonder, what is she looking at? What is she trying to say?"[13]

Ghosts in the Mirror

Another way that ghosts can make themselves known is in a mirror. There have been many reports of people who have seen the faces of the dead in mirrors. For centuries in England and parts of the United States, mirrors would be covered immediately after the death of a family member, lest a spirit be tempted to return to Earth.

Sometimes an unusual mirror image was seen as an omen. Abraham Lincoln, who believed in the existence of ghosts, saw a double image of himself in the mirror shortly before he was elected president in 1860. One image was his normal self, but the other upset him. This second image was a clearly ill Lincoln, pale and sickly—almost deathlike. The mirror image upset Lincoln, who believed that it was a premonition. The unhealthy appearance of the second image, he believed, meant he would die during his second term in office. Interestingly, his premonition proved true, when he was shot and killed in April 1865, during his second term in office.

Author Tom Ogden tells of a female friend in the U.S. embassy in Argentina who had a very upsetting experience with a mirror. The woman, who Ogden says is levelheaded and very rational, confided to him that she owned what she was certain was a haunted wall mirror. It had belonged to her grandmother, who had left it to her in her will. When she first hung it on the wall, the woman said that she would occasionally glimpse the form of an elderly woman as she passed by. "But sometimes," Ogden recalls, "she would see the unmistakable face of her grandmother peering out at her. The ghost didn't try to communicate with her in any way and expressed no emotion—neither happiness, sorrow, or pain."[14]

Not surprisingly, the woman was frightened by the image, but was left with a problem. Her first instinct was to destroy the mirror, but if her grandmother's spirit was somehow trapped inside it, she wondered, what would happen to that spirit? She decided instead to place the mirror in storage—forever.

Doubles

Another mysterious type of ghost is known as a doppelgänger, a German word meaning "double-walker." A doppelgänger is basically an exact double of a living person. Seeing a doppelgänger was thought to be a harbinger of one's own death. The young poet Percy Bysshe Shelley was frightened when he saw his doppelgänger in Italy. The spirit stared at him for a moment and, without speaking, pointed at the Mediterranean Sea. Weeks afterward, Shelley drowned in a boating accident.

John Donne, another famous poet, saw a doppelgänger in 1612— not his own but that of his wife. It appeared to him while he was

A doppelgänger is basically an exact double of a living person. Seeing a doppelgänger was thought to be a harbinger of one's own death. The young poet Percy Bysshe Shelley was frightened when he saw his doppelgänger in Italy. He died weeks later.

in Paris, although he knew his wife was in England about to give birth to their child. The spirit was clearly grieving, but he did not understand why. It would not speak to him but merely stood in his chambers, looking forlorn. He learned later that at the time the spirit appeared to him, his wife had delivered a stillborn baby.

The Teacher and the Doppelgänger

One of the most well-reported cases of a doppelgänger was reported in 1854 by an American writer named Robert Dale Owen.

Unlike other doppelgängers, this spirit double was not an omen of death but it frayed nerves nonetheless. It centered around a young French woman named Emilie Sagee.

Sagee was a teacher in an exclusive girls' school in Latvia at the time. Sagee was the subject of a great deal of speculation among students and faculty at the school, for she had an exact double that would appear and disappear in full view of her pupils. In class one day, for example, as Sagee wrote out exercises on the blackboard, her doppelgänger appeared next to her. It, too, went through the motions of writing on the blackboard, although it held no chalk in its hand.

On another occasion, the students assembled in the school's main hall for sewing and embroidery lessons. As the girls worked on their projects, some looked out the window and saw Sagee working in the garden. But others saw Sagee's double in the hall, seated in a chair supervising their sewing. Two of the braver girls approached the double and tried to touch it, but later reported that they "felt an odd resistance in the air."[15]

Interestingly, though scores of witnesses saw Sagee's doppelgänger, she herself never did. She did say that when the double was said to have appeared, she felt listless and drained of energy. And while the doppelgänger caused no trouble, it caused Sagee to lose several teaching positions. Students' stories about their teacher alarmed enough parents that the school's administration felt it was best to fire Sagee.

On January 27, 1967, three Apollo astronauts, (left to right) Lieutenant Colonel Virgil Grissom, Lieutenant Colonel Edward White, and Lieutenant Commander Roger Chafee died in a cabin fire on Launch Pad #34. The platform has since been abandoned, but stories of ghastly screams continue to circulate.

Biblical Ghosts

Ghosts are mentioned in the Old Testament of the Bible, too. King Saul, an early leader of the Israelites, needed advice on an upcoming battle. Although it was against religious law in those days to consult with wizards or fortune-tellers in order to contact ghosts, Saul was desperate. He traveled to another region where he would not be recognized and asked a fortune-teller to call up the ghost of the prophet, Samuel. Although the fortune-teller was able to summon the spirit, Samuel's ghost was furious at being disturbed and refused to help Saul.

The Sounds of Ghosts

In many cases ghosts are believed to make themselves known by sounds rather than by visible appearances. In London, for example, an orphanage burned down in the late 1880s. It is believed that seven children were killed in the fire. Though the site of the fire is now a bookstore, many people have heard what they insist

*Many ghost
researchers
say that battle-
fields—where
sudden, violent
death occurred
by the hun-
dreds or even
thousands—are
places where
ghost activity
is frequently
reported. The
Civil War Battle
of Antietam, for
example, left
thousands of
soldiers dead.*

are the sounds of small children crying and screaming late at night. Many think that the sounds are the cries of the children who could not escape the fire more than a century ago.

Another deadly fire is said to have created a haunted place, this one at Launch Pad #34 at the Kennedy Space Center. On January 27, 1967, 3 Apollo astronauts, Lieutenant Colonel Virgil Grissom, Lieutenant Commander Roger Chafee, and Lieutenant Colonel Edward White, were going through a preparation test 2 weeks before their space mission. The test resulted in tragedy when a short circuit in some wiring caused a spark in the cabin where the men were seated. Because the cabin was filled with pure oxygen, a raging fire quickly engulfed the cabin, killing all 3.

That launch pad was later abandoned by space officials, who scheduled take-offs from other areas at the complex. However, strange stories began to circulate about that particular area. Workers reported hearing spine-chilling yells and screams at night and in the early morning hours. One former security guard at Kennedy Space Center clearly recalls something very strange happening at Launch Pad #34:

> Everybody talked about it being haunted. I mean, after all, look at what happened there: three astronauts burned up. I used to patrol that area, and I'd always get an eerie feeling out there . . . especially at night. I've heard a few guys say they'd heard screams there, yet there would be no sign of anyone. Of course, nobody ever made an official report, or they would've been called loony. [16]

Dieppe, a coastal town of France, was occupied by the Nazis early in World War II. On August 19, 1942, a bloody battle occurred when Allied forces made up of mostly British and Canadian troops attempted to liberate Dieppe. The operation failed, and 6,000 Allied soldiers were killed—cut down by machine-gun fire as they landed on the beach. People have reportedly heard unexplained sounds like gunfire, screams, and planes since the battle.

The Echoes of Battle

Many ghost researchers say that battlefields—where sudden, violent death occurred by the hundreds or even thousands—are places where ghost activity is frequently reported. In the United States ghostly noises have been heard at many of the Civil War battlefields. At Gettysburg, Pennsylvania, where thousands of soldiers died during a four-day battle in July 1863, many visitors have heard the sound of military drumming early in the morning. Others have reported hearing shouting and the clanking of swords on the empty battlefield.

World War II battlegrounds have had ghost reports, too. One was at Dieppe, a coastal town of France, which was occupied by the Nazis early in the war. Just before dawn on August 19, 1942, a bloody battle occurred when Allied forces made up of mostly British and Canadian troops attempted to liberate Dieppe. The operation failed, and 6,000 Allied soldiers were killed—cut down by machine-gun fire as they landed on the beach.

In August 1951 an Englishwoman and her sister-in-law were vacationing in Puys, a little village near Dieppe. They woke early one morning to loud noises coming from the beach. For 20 minutes they listened to what they later reported as gunfire, the sounds of planes dive-bombing, and screams. Over the next couple of hours, they said, the noises stopped then started again. Though the noises were loud and seemed very close the women could see nothing.

After reporting their experience, the women learned that the beach in Puys had been one of the Allied landing points in the failed raid. They also learned that the times they heard the noises coincided with the times that the battle had taken place nine years before. Historical researchers interviewed the women and found them credible. The British Society of Psychical Research, which investigates many claims of ghostly activity, had no definitive explanation but declared in 1953 that "the experience must be rated as a genuine psychic experience."[17]

Another Question

It is clear from the thousands of people who have experienced what they believe to be ghost activity that spirits can make their presence known to the living in many ways. As people throughout history have unintentionally come into contact with what seem to be the spirits of the dead, however, they wonder why those ghosts have not moved on to the spirit world. Trying to answer that question can be a fascinating challenge.

CHAPTER 2

Why Spirits Remain

The ghost that haunted Athenodorus's house in ancient times was restless because he had not been properly buried. This story is just one of thousands of accounts of spirits who have the same reason for remaining on Earth. They are restless and often angry that their remains have not been handled with dignity and respect.

"We tend to think of funerals as being for the living," says Grace Donne, a ghost researcher, "but when we look at the reasons spirits do not cross over [into the spirit world], it may actually be just as important to the spirit of the deceased. For those spirits, the funeral ceremony is a way for them to know that their time on earth is over, that they were loved, but that they no longer reside here."[18]

Rows of the Unburied

Other researchers agree. They point to the large number of spirits that are reported to linger at battlefields or the sites of disasters. At many of these sites people had neither time nor opportunity to give the bodies of the dead traditional burials.

In late December 2004, for example, a devastating tsunami struck Indonesia, Sri Lanka, and Thailand. More than a quarter of a million people were killed as the powerful waves destroyed entire towns. Another 70,000 were missing and believed dead—either drowned and carried out to sea, or their bodies so unrecognizable that they could not be identified by family members.

Because of the sheer numbers of dead, when bodies were recovered they were laid outside in long rows. Authorities hoped that survivors would come to claim their dead loved ones so they could be buried. But as the days and weeks went on, many thousands of victims remained in the long rows. In some cases the dead included whole families, leaving no one to collect their remains. In other cases the heat had caused the bodies to decompose to the point that they could not be easily identified.

"The Ghosts Are a Problem"

As a result, few funerals took place. Survivors told of many ghostly encounters in areas hit by the tsunami. Wrote one reporter in Thailand, "The grapevine is alive with ghost stories: the fisherman on Phi Phi Island who heard a large group of Westerners calling for help but when he looked he saw nobody; the tuk tuk [taxi] driver who stopped for five tourists, . . . then, when he looked behind him into the tuk-tuk, found no passengers."[19]

"The funeral ceremony is a way for [the dead] to know that their time on earth is over."

—Ghost researcher explaining the importance of funerals for the dead.

People living in areas hit by the tsunami of 2004 believed they were seeing and hearing the spirits of tsunami victims who had not been buried. They worried that such ghosts would cause trouble for the living.

Ghosts

People living in these areas believed they were seeing and hearing the spirits of tsunami victims who had not been buried. They worried that such ghosts would cause trouble for the living, that they would bring bad luck and poor health. One Thai woman said that the large number of ghosts near her home caused her to leave the area permanently. "The ghosts are a problem," she said. "Thai people hate ghosts, and Phuket [an island especially hard hit by the tsunami] is full of them. I won't go down there again."[20]

A Final Goodbye

Lack of proper burial is only one reason for ghosts' remaining on Earth. Sometimes ghosts have other reasons for postponing the journey to the spirit world. In many cases, at the moment of a person's death, his or her ghost appears to a loved one. Ghost researchers say that such appearances are very short. Witnesses say the spirit often does not even speak but just maintains eye contact with the loved one—perhaps to have one more look before moving on to the spirit world.

Jen, a piano teacher living in Fargo, North Dakota, says that she was visited by the spirit of her brother in 1968, during the Vietnam War. "It was a long time ago," she says.

> We were living in Minneapolis then. I was eighteen; my brother A. J. was four years older. He was serving in Vietnam, and my family was so worried about him. The news every night was frightening—so many American boys were being killed over there.
>
> The day he appeared to me, I'd been at the beach

with friends and then out for dinner. It was my best friend's birthday, June 21st. I remember A.J. was in my thoughts a lot that day because we were doing stuff he loved to do—water skiing, hanging out, just enjoying the summer. I was thinking it was going to be so great when he finally got to come home.[21]

"A.J., What's Happening?"

That night, Jen says she woke suddenly after being asleep for only a few minutes.

> I woke up fast, like when you hear someone calling your name, you know? And there he was, standing by the dresser in my room. I remember saying, "A.J., what's happening? Why didn't you tell us you were coming home?"
>
> He was standing there in his uniform, just standing there. He just smiled at me. And then, I don't know, it was like he wasn't there. It was one of those weird things where you are sure something happened, but then you doubt yourself. It didn't feel like a dream at all—that I'm sure of."[22]

Jen says that several days later, two uniformed officers came to their door to tell her mother and father that A. J. had been killed while on patrol. It had happened the day she saw him in her room. "He was dead when he appeared to me," says Jen. "Even now, more than forty years later, it rattles me, thinking about it."[23]

A Stranger's Thank You

It is not always family members who have experienced these quick appearances by spirits at the moment of death. Ghost investigator Linda Zimmermann interviewed a New York police officer named Jim Janso. He had been on the scene at a traffic accident in May 1999—an accident that police and other emergency workers ranked as the worst they had ever seen.

Two large trucks had hit head-on, and while one driver was killed immediately, the other was close to death, trapped in the wreckage. The driver was distressed and confused, and Janso did not want him to die alone. He stayed with the driver, talking quietly to him, hoping to calm him down. After emergency crews were able to free him from the twisted metal of his truck, the man died.

That night, Janso told Zimmermann, he tossed and turned, unable to get to sleep. In the middle of the night when he turned to look at his nightstand clock, he had a tremendous shock. Standing just a few feet away was the truck driver he had stayed with. But he looked different—healthy and whole. His clothes were no longer bloody and stained, but clean. "As Janso stared, the man smiled at him and said, 'Thank you.'"[24] Then he was gone.

Janso explained that he told very few people about his experience. Like many who have seen a ghost, he knew most people would not believe him. Even so, he felt better knowing that the driver's spirit was not worried or restless and could move on to the spirit world after expressing his gratitude.

Helping Hands

Many have reported other ghosts who seem to have remained because they feel that they can still be of help to the living. Randall Barnes of Arlington, Illinois, says that when he was in

"He was dead when he appeared to me."

— A woman commenting on her brother's strange appearance to her after he'd been killed in Vietnam.

college in the late 1980s, he had an experience with such a ghost. In fact, he says, without that ghost's help, he would not have passed his math class.

The night before the final, Barnes and his girlfriend were studying in the library, but not very successfully. "We were both under a lot of stress," Barnes recalls, "because we just couldn't seem to understand some of the basic principles involved in solving certain math problems."[25]

By 3:00 A.M. the two of them were about ready to give up in frustration, when an elderly man suddenly walked up to their table. White-haired and dressed in a dark suit with a floppy, polka-dot tie, the man introduced himself as Professor Martin, who had taught mathematics at the college for many years. He offered to help them, and for the next two hours the professor went through the material with them. It was clear that he had been an extraordinary teacher with a knack for making even the most difficult problems easy.

Success—and a Shock

Later that day, after taking the final and confident that they had done extremely well, the two students decided to send a letter to Martin, thanking him for his help. They went to the administration building to get his address, but the secretary was confused.

She told them that they must have gotten the name wrong. The only Martin that had taught mathematics there had died in

1963, more than 20 years before. To prove her point, she showed them a yearbook picture of Martin. It was the same man, even down to the floppy, polka-dot tie.

Wondering if their late night studying had made them imagine the entire episode, the two asked their math teacher if he had known Martin. He had, and told them that over the years since Martin's death, several students had encountered him in the library and received his help with math. Happiest when teaching and helping young people, Martin had evidently decided not to cross over to the spirit world.

Warnings

Sometimes helpful ghosts are believed to appear to the living in an effort to atone for mistakes made during their lives. One of the eeriest of these cases involves the crew of an Eastern Airlines flight that crashed on December 29, 1972. Flight 401 was flying nonstop from New York to Miami when it crashed in the Florida Everglades.

Though the pilot and other members of the crew had a great deal of experience, they encountered a problem with their equipment just as they were making their approach to the Miami airport. An important light on the instrument panel did not go on, and while trying to determine the cause of the problem, the pilot and his crew did not realize that the plane was losing altitude. By the time they saw what was happening, it was too late. The plane crashed, and 100 passengers and crew were killed—including pilot Bob Loft and flight engineer Don Repo.

Soon after the crash Eastern Airlines salvaged what was left of the plane. Some of the parts were tested to make certain they were undamaged and then put into other planes in the Eastern fleet. But in the weeks and months afterward, some frightening things began occurring on these other planes.

"Oh My God, It's Bob Loft!"

Some crews working on these planes began experiencing odd sensations. Sometimes it was an unexplained cold spot. In other cases, flight attendants working in the galley felt that they were being watched when no one else was around. But the most frightening were the appearances of two men on these airplanes—the dead pilot and flight engineer of Flight 401.

One flight attendant was preparing food for passengers when she saw the unmistakable image of a face staring at her from the glass door of a warming oven. She recognized it as the face of Repo, the flight engineer who had been trying to solve the equipment malfunction problem when Flight 401 crashed. Shaken, she ran to tell a coworker. The second flight attendant went to look. She, too, saw a face in the door. They asked the flight engineer to take a look. He not only saw the image, but it spoke to him. Repo said, "Watch out for fire on this airplane,"[26] and vanished. Shortly afterward, the plane was taking off from Mexico City when it developed a fire in one of its engines. The crew was able to quickly land the plane without incident.

Before another flight, an attendant noticed a uniformed pilot in the first class section who appeared to be flying as a passenger en route to work. However, when she spoke with him, he stared straight ahead and never spoke. Other attendants had the same experience. Concerned, they asked their own pilot to come back to talk with the man. When he leaned down to speak to the man, he was aghast. "My God," he said, "it's Bob Loft!"[27] The only explanation appeared to be that these planes had ghosts.

On December 29, 1972, Flight 401 was flying from New York to Miami when it crashed in the Florida Everglades. Soon after the crash Eastern Airlines salvaged what was left of the plane. Some of the parts were tested to make certain they were undamaged and then put into other planes in the Eastern fleet. Many of these planes reported strange happenings.

Helping Avoid More Disasters

The sightings increased, occurring on several planes that had parts from Flight 401. Though both ghosts made appearances, Repo's ghost was seen more often. He seemed to be especially concerned with the safety of the plane. He was reported as doing preflight instrument checks, making sure all of them were in working order—as they had *not* been for the doomed 401. On several occasions, flight crews said, Repo's ghost warned them about potential problems on their planes. Ghost researchers speculated that he felt guilt about the crash of 401 and remained on Earth to help prevent other accidents.

Though many crew members claimed to have seen the ghosts, the stories were hard to believe. Eastern Airlines management was especially skeptical. One flight attendant said that she and others were told by airline officials that they should see a psychiatrist. Worried that they would be viewed as unstable, they stopped talking about the sightings. "So very few will talk about the story any more," she told one interviewer. "A lot [of the crew members] feel they'll be fired or laid off."[28]

But the sightings worried management, who were concerned that their planes would get the reputation of being haunted. Eventually, they ordered that all parts recycled from Flight 401 be replaced. Shortly afterward, all sightings of Repo and Loft stopped.

The Unsure Dead

While the spirits of Repo and Loft seemed to have had a mission in remaining on Earth, in a large number of cases ghosts remain on Earth simply because they are confused. They may not realize that they are no longer living—especially if their deaths occurred quickly and unexpectedly. Battlefields, for example, are rumored to be filled with the confused ghosts of those whose lives ended so abruptly that they did not understand they were dead—and so continued to fight the battle in which they were engaged at the moment they were killed.

Gettysburg, Pennsylvania, was the site of a three-day battle during the Civil War that resulted in more deaths than any other battle. Nearly 8,000 soldiers were killed between July 1 and July 3, 1863, and 45,000 more were wounded. Visitors and residents alike have heard phantom soldiers, unaware that they are no longer living, walking the fields where the battles took place, searching for their friends and fellow soldiers. Many visitors say they had the eerie feeling that they were being watched. Some spotted raggedy soldiers behind trees or even gathering wood for a fire. The images disappeared after a few seconds.

Meeting a Confederate Ghost

One incident occurred in July 1993 at the 130th anniversary of the Battle of Gettysburg. A group of reenactors (Civil War experts who dress in authentic-looking uniforms to dramatize war events for others) were relaxing after the day's events. Dressed as Confederate soldiers, they took a walk to Little Round Top, a small hill that was the site of one of the Gettysburg battles. As they sat just enjoying the evening, they suddenly saw another man dressed as a Confederate soldier walking toward them. They were startled, for they had not seen or heard his approach.

The man, they all noticed, was wearing one of the most authentic-looking uniforms they had ever seen. It was in poor condition, too—sweat-stained and marked with what looked very much like blood on the left shoulder. The soldier himself looked like an

Ghosts

In July 1993 at the one hundred thirtieth anniversary of the Battle of Gettysburg, a group of re-enactors was relaxing after the day's events when they were approached by the ghost of a Confederate soldier. Here, Confederate re-enactors reload their rifles as others prepare a canon to be fired during a Civil War reenactment battle in Indiana. This group is wearing replicas of the traditional Confederate uniform.

authentic soldier of the period, with black stains on his teeth from biting off the paper cartridges to pour the gunpowder into the barrel of his rifle. He greeted the reenactors and reached into his cartridge box and handed them each a cartridge, telling them that the ammunition would come in handy the next day.

He walked away, and the men examined the cartridges. They were amazingly real—as if they had been made by a real soldier of the Civil War—paper filled with gunpowder, tied carefully with a thread, and sealed on one end with a bit of beeswax. What astonished them most, however, was that each of the cartridges contained a minié ball—the soft lead bullet loaded into the muzzles of Civil War–era rifles. Minié balls were rare antiques and would never have been used by reenactors, who could not carry live ammunition.

The men jumped to their feet and tried to find the soldier, but it was as if he had simply vanished. Their feeling that they might have seen a Confederate ghost was supported by the Gettysburg museum director days later. She determined that the cartridges were not copies but were authentic Civil War ammunition. The Confederate soldier had to have been real—at least his spirit was.

Resurrection Mary

Sometimes ghost researchers have no ready explanations for why some spirits stay. That is the case with the most famous ghost in the Chicago area, a pretty young blonde woman known as Resurrection Mary. She has been seen by hundreds of people since her first appearance in the 1930s.

Although no one is certain of her real name, she is believed to have been killed in an accident on Chicago's South Side. According to legend, she and a boyfriend had gone to the Willowbrook Ballroom for an evening of dancing. While there, however, she and her boyfriend quarreled, and she left, preferring to hitchhike home rather than spend any more time with her date. But as she stood on the side of the rode, she was struck by a passing car and killed. She was believed to have been buried in Resurrection Cemetery, near which her spirit roams.

Soon after her death police began getting reports of sightings of a young woman in an evening dress hitchhiking on busy Archer Avenue. If any passing motorist who stopped to give her a ride—often a cab driver—asked where she was going, she would tell him just to keep driving on Archer. Eventually she would tell him to pull over. When he did, he would notice that it was the entrance to Resurrection Cemetery. As he would turn to ask her why she wanted to get off there, he would realize he was alone in the car. Over the years the sightings increased. People of all ages and occupations reported seeing her—cab drivers, teachers, doctors, and even a deacon of the Greek Orthodox Church.

Hit and Run

Beginning in the 1960s the reports about Resurrection Mary changed. Not only was she seen hitchhiking on Archer Avenue, but she would occasionally jump out in front of a passing car and would be struck. When the frantic drivers stopped, they could find no trace of a body.

Chet Prusinski, the owner of a bar near Resurrection Cemetery, used to tell about a man who came running into the bar at 4:00 A.M. just as Prusinski was leaving. The man was in distress—he said he needed to use the telephone. He had hit a girl walking on the road, but now could not find her body. Prusinski

Ouija Boards

Though many people think of Ouija boards as a game, many spiritualists use them to contact spirits. Two people put their fingertips on a small stand called a planchette. When the two concentrate very hard on a ghost or spirit, the planchette moves over the letters of the board, spelling out messages from the spirit world. Many psychics believe that Ouija boards are dangerous, for they call up spirits that may be dangerous or evil.

was skeptical about the story until a truck driver came in. He had seen the accident and verified the man's story. But as before, when the police arrived, there was no body to be found.

Troy Taylor, who has written extensively about ghosts and other paranormal events, was contacted in July 2001 by a man who had recently seen Resurrection Mary on Archer Avenue. She was carrying a bouquet of dark flowers and was walking just north of the cemetery. She suddenly stopped and stared at the witness, who had stopped his car to get a better look at her. "She wasn't looking at us," he told Taylor. "She was just staring to the south. She looked somewhat young with the blankest expression I have ever seen on her face."[29]

Scary but Harmless

As with many others who have experienced sightings of Resurrection Mary in Chicago, the man admitted that the encounter caused him to change his driving habits. "After that July, I refuse to drive by the cemetery alone," he says. "I take another route if I ever have to go that way."[30]

Resurrection Mary has never shown any signs of being angry or dangerous. In that way she is like the large majority of ghosts. However, to assume that all spirits are harmless would be a mistake. In fact, another category of spirits is known for being very much the opposite.

CHAPTER 3

Poltergeists

One particular type of spirit has made its presence known for as long as other ghosts have but in far more menacing ways. Through the centuries various cultures have had their own names for it, but today it is known most commonly by its German name, poltergeist, which means "noisy ghost."

Poltergeists do not make themselves visible as other ghosts do. However, they are far more active than other ghosts. And of all the various types of ghosts, says ghost researcher Peter Underwood, "these are probably the most unpleasant." Underwood says that poltergeists have long been viewed as "malevolent entities who seem to take delight in persecuting innocent people."[31]

Pinch, Poke, Slap, Crash

Poltergeists have a variety of tricks. Sometimes they just make a lot of noise, bothering and frightening people with a series of bangs and thuds late at night. In one house in Fort Wayne, Indiana, poltergeists were suggested as the cause of the sound of

Poltergeists have a variety of tricks. Sometimes they just make a lot of noise, bothering and frightening people with a series of bangs and thuds late at night. In one house in Fort Wayne, Indiana, poltergeists were suggested as the cause of the sound of Ping-Pong balls being bounced on the floor of an upstairs room.

Ping-Pong balls being bounced on the floor of an upstairs room. The couple who lived in the house had no children and were using the room for storage. There was no explanation for the sounds of the Ping-Pong balls, and the couple eventually moved because the noise would not stop.

"We couldn't sleep," says Julius, who asked that his last name not be used.

> It wasn't all night. It wasn't every night, either. But it was often enough, and loud enough, to where we were like the walking dead in the morning. I was tired of running upstairs several times a night. There [was] never anything there. We had people come in and spend some time, and they

heard it, too. They recorded it, and we all agreed, it was definitely Ping-Pong balls. I figured if my wife and I were hearing things, then these guys with their tape recorder were, too. I'm glad to be out of there—I was glad we were renting the place and didn't have to worry about selling it.[32]

Other people have complained of physical contact in addition to the noises. Some say they have been slapped or punched or even woken up from a deep sleep after being pinched on the legs. Sometimes victims find bruises or red marks afterward.

Pelted by Rocks

Another way poltergeists have been reported to frighten people is by hurling rocks. The first recorded case of what experts believe was poltergeist activity occurred in A.D. 858 in the German town Bingen-on-Rhine. Residents were astonished when their whole town began being pelted by rocks. They had no explanation, nor had the townspeople ever heard of such a thing happening before.

In some cases the bizarre rock showers have even rained down *inside* homes. In 1903 W.G. Grotten-Dieck, a Dutch oil explorer living on the island of Sumatra in Indonesia, awoke to the sound of something falling on the floor nearby. What he saw, he later told the British Society of Psychical Research (SPR), astonished him. "They were black stones from an eighth to three-quarters of an inch long," he said. "I got out of the [mosquito] curtain and turned up the kerosene lamp that was standing on the floor at the foot of my bed. . . . [The stones] fell on the floor, close to my head-pillow."[33]

"I Could Never Catch Them"

Grotten-Dieck yelled to awaken his house servant who was sleeping in the next room. He sent the young man outside to find the source of the falling rocks. The servant came back inside, finding no rocks falling in the jungle outside. Grotten-Dieck, meanwhile, found that the rocks that landed around him were somewhat warm to the touch, which he found curious. Something else was strange about the falling rocks, and he reported this to the SPR:

"I knelt down near [the head of my bed] and tried to catch the stones while they were falling through the air towards me, but I could never catch them. It seemed to me that they changed their direction in the air as soon as I tried to get hold of them. I could not catch any of them before they fell on the floor." Grotten-Dieck reported that he fired five shots into the jungle, hoping to kill whoever was responsible for the frightening event. However, the shooting appeared to have the opposite effect. "The stones, far from stopping," he said, "fell even more abundantly after my shots than before."[34]

A Poltergeist in California

Some cases of rock throwing have continued on and off for weeks or months. A family from Big Bear, California, fled their home because of ongoing episodes. On and off for four months in 1962, showers of rocks fell on their home. As in the Grotten-Dieck case, the rocks felt surprisingly warm. And they appeared to fall at an angle, almost like snow. The family noticed that the rocks seemed to almost float as they came down.

Even though the rock showers resulted in no serious injuries, the episodes were frightening. The family worked with the San Bernardino Sheriff's Department, trying to find an explanation

Not Feathers and Crystals

Many people are embarrassed to seek help when they have unexplained phenomena in their homes. Julius, who asked that his last name not be used, rented a house in Fort Wayne, Indiana. He and his wife experienced what were believed to be poltergeists in 2004. Julius did not believe in ghosts then and says he was relieved when a research team arrived with electronic equipment. "I guess I thought it would be feathers or crystals or something," he says. "But it was cameras and tape recorders—normal stuff."

Julius, telephone interview with author, July 15, 2007.

but had little success. Some theories were explored, such as meteor showers or people firing rocks at the house with slingshots.

But no meteor showers in the vicinity had been reported, and no evidence of people hurling rocks at the home could be found. After investigating as thoroughly as they could, the sheriff's department could find no explanation for the episodes.

A Person, Not a Place

Some researchers have noted other differences between poltergeists and other ghosts besides the aggressive nature of their actions. Ghosts, they say, tend to be attached to places. Whether in a house, on a battlefield, or along a stretch of road, a ghost tends to stay in one general location. A poltergeist, however, seems to be attached to a particular person. The majority of episodes occur when that person is nearby.

That was the case in 1958 when the Herrmann family began experiencing some strange activities in their Long Island, New York, home. There were no rock showers in the Herrmann house, but beginning on February 3, bottles throughout the home were popping their caps for no apparent reason. The bottles were of the twist-top sort, which would need three or four turns to remove them. But the tops were popping off, causing little explosions. It began with bottles of perfume, bleach, and nail polish. The top even exploded off a small bottle containing holy water.

At first, the Herrmanns wondered if their 12-year-old son Jimmy was involved. He was often present when the explosions occurred, although they never saw him do anything suspicious. But as time went by, they were convinced he had nothing to do with it. Once, James Herrmann was in the bathroom when his son was brushing his teeth. He watched as a shampoo bottle and a medicine bottle moved on their own power across the basin and crashed into the sink. Herrmann realized his son was blameless.

Calling the Police

The incidents got more and more aggressive as the weeks went by. A porcelain figurine appeared to hurl itself against a wooden desk, denting it. A bottle of ink seemed to fly from the dining room table and shattered against the front door. Herrmann called the police, hoping that they could find an explanation for what was becoming a very unsettling situation.

Detective Joseph Tozzi, the officer assigned to the case, had a reputation for being cynical and very persistent. He was not the sort of person who would take Herrmann's word that his son was innocent. He would make up his own mind once he saw exactly what was going on.

It did not take long for Tozzi to realize that there was a big problem in the Herrmanns' home. The first day he was there, he witnessed several objects moving on their own. He checked for strings or other methods someone could use for moving things without appearing to do so. He found nothing. The second day, he was inspecting the basement of the house, and as he and James were walking downstairs, a heavy bronze figurine suddenly flew across the basement and hit Tozzi in the legs.

Eliminating Natural Causes

Tozzi kept on the case. He decided to try eliminating possible natural causes. Perhaps the air force base nearby was causing unusual shock waves, or radio waves were creating bizarre effects. But officials at Michel Air Force Base insisted nothing they were doing could be responsible. And electricians found nothing out of the ordinary.

The story leaked to the press, and soon everyone had an opinion. Many believed it was Jimmy, but Tozzi was certain he was innocent. Some suggested a ghost, but Tozzi was not ready to accept that either. No one ever figured out the cause of the strange occurrences in the Herrmann home. But by March 1958 the episodes in the house began lessening, and on March 10 they stopped altogether.

David Kahn, a newspaper reporter who covered the case, was more open than Tozzi to the idea of a ghost being responsible. "When asked what the answer is," Kahn said in 2007, looking back almost 50 years, "I say that all we can do is class the events as an instance of a poltergeist and await an explanation of the phenomenon."[35]

More Deadly than Popping Bottles

Though the Herrmann case fits many other poltergeist episodes, in other cases the poltergeist activity is far more dangerous than breaking dishes and popping the tops from bottles. One of the most famous poltergeist cases in the United States occurred in Macomb, Illinois, in 1948. It lasted for only three weeks but resulted in a great deal of destruction. The weapon with which the Macomb poltergeist caused trouble was fire.

As with most poltergeist occurrences, this one seemed to be centered on one person—a 13-year-old named Wanet McNeill. After her parents divorced, she and her father moved to the farm of her uncle, Charles Willey. On August 7 unexplained fires began. They began as little dark brown spots on the wallpaper of the farmhouse. Then they would mysteriously burst into flames.

The little fires became a daily occurrence, and family and neighbors came to help keep a vigil, watching the walls and ceiling in fascination as the brown spots spontaneously appeared and began to smolder. They kept saucepans and buckets of water throughout the house to put the fires out quickly. Over the next week 200 such fires broke out—an average of 29 each day. On August 14, a week after the fires began, so many broke out at the same time, the house burned to the ground. The following day the barn burned down, too.

A Bogus Confession?

As the family moved to a vacant house nearby, police conducted their investigation. They ruled out natural causes, such as a gas leak or radiation from an unseen source. They began to consider the fires as arson and considered Wanet a likely suspect. On August 30, after an hour-long intensive interrogation, authorities announced that the girl had confessed. They said she told them about setting the fires with ordinary kitchen matches because she hated living on the farm.

But few people believed the girl's confession. The doubters included family members and neighbors, those police who were at the scene, and a newspaper reporter. They insisted that she could not have set the fires. As researcher Troy Taylor explains, the girl's confession did not make sense to paranormal experts who knew the facts of the case. "Forgotten," he said, "were the witnesses who had seen the brown spots appear, spread, and then turn into fires while Wanet was nowhere to be seen."[36] Instead of investigating the idea of a paranormal event, law enforcement decided that a confession, no matter how nonsensical, could provide the end to what was an unsettling time in the community.

Studying Poltergeists

Gathering data on possible poltergeist activity is not an easy task, however. As a result, researchers estimate that only 12 percent of such cases are reported or investigated. One reason is that a poltergeist incident tends to be short-lived—typically from a week or two to a few months. By the time most families decide the activity is out of their control, it tends to diminish and then disappear.

Some ghosts, such as a poltergeists, can display angry behavior and attempt to harm people. The person in this illustration is frightened by a ghost.

Even more problematic is that most people are reluctant to report such strange happenings in their homes. "Reporting of the occurrences is rare," notes parapsychologist William Roll of Duke

University, "because people tend to think they are possessed or they are afraid of being accused of being crazy. So you don't get a lot of people coming forward."[37]

Over the years ghost researchers have arrived at very different theories about what poltergeists are. Centuries ago people believed that a person around whom poltergeist-type activity took place was a witch or demon. But in the 1950s researcher Hereward Carrington noted that a young person at the onset of puberty was almost always the center, or agent, of such activity. Carrington thought that the physical and emotional stress of puberty, in combination with other unknown factors, caused the disruptions. Agents were responsible for the activity but were unaware they were the cause. He said that in these young people "an energy seems to be radiated from the body. . . . It would almost seem as though these energies, instead of taking their normal course . . . find this curious method of externalization."[38]

"I Should Have Five at My House"

While some felt Carrington's theory had merit, others were skeptical. Puberty and the stress it produces are far too common to suggest such an uncommon event as poltergeist activity. If it were true, they said, why was every household with a teenager not experiencing rock showers or fires? Every teen experiences stress, and each experiences surges of hormones during puberty.

This theory seemed too simplistic to many researchers, but other theories used this one as a starting point. Some researchers have noted that many poltergeist cases revolve around teens with more than the typical teenage stress. Some may be in families going through divorce or other family upheaval. Some agents have been found to be victims of emotional or sexual abuse. Instead of acting out the anger they feel, these teens may repress, or bottle up, their feelings. As a result, these feelings could come out unconsciously as loud or destructive poltergeist actions.

Interfering with Gravity?

Roll, having interviewed more agents than anyone else has, is considered to be a pioneer in American poltergeist research. He has theorized that the brain of an agent may have an unusual physical aspect. Whatever it is, he says, may allow the agent to unconsciously interfere with gravity, thereby causing objects to levitate, or float through the air. "It's still speculation," he said in a 2005 interview. "But I think something interferes with inertia [the law of physics that says an object at rest tends to remain at rest] and gravity."[39]

A Poltergeist in Kentucky

Roll investigated a case involving levitation in Olive Hill, Kentucky, in 1968. The agent appeared to be 12-year-old Roger Callihan, living with his family at the home of his grandparents. Witnesses saw glass statues levitate and shatter; they also saw furniture move by itself. One friend of the family says she visited the house and saw a heavy table in the air, following Roger as he walked toward her.

Every time there was an occurrence, Roger was nearby. Even though it would have been virtually impossible for Roger to lift or throw heavy tables and chairs, his family kept a close eye on him. Never once did they see him do anything suspicious.

When Roll visited the home, he witnessed the levitation firsthand. "At one point," Roll recalled later, "I was following Roger, walking right behind him into the kitchen, when the kitchen table jumped into the air, rotated 45 degrees and fell down on the backs of the chairs that stood around it, its four legs off the floor. Roger and the table were in full view."[40]

Roll thought the onset of puberty and the stress of living away from home had probably contributed to these bizarre events. But he also believed that Roger had some physical oddity that allowed such unbelievable events to occur.

A New Kind of Psychokinesis?

Other researchers have suggested that the levitation is caused by some type of psychokinesis (PK), a paranormal ability that enables some people to move objects using their minds. Though rare, there have been cases of psychokinesis in which people appear to be able to bend metal keys or spoons or turn pages of books simply by concentrating their minds on these objects.

Some poltergeist researchers say that agents may be using a type of PK that does not come from concentration but occurs subconsciously because of stress, hormonal changes, and other factors. They have termed this paranormal ability RSPK, short for "recurrent spontaneous psychokinesis."

Many skeptics believe that neither PK nor RSPK have any basis in fact. They claim that psychic spoon bending and other such feats are fraudulent. However, many people are not so quick to write off PK. Some, such as Minnesota surgeon Paul Johnson says that the mind's ability to control matter is evident every day. "I know that the mind can control a great deal," he says. "I tell a lot of my stressed-out patients to take up yoga or other type of meditation. It can lower your blood pressure and lessen the effects of stress in a lot of ways. We've known that for years."[41]

Underwood agrees. He says that it is possible for the mind to have even more unusual effects on the body. In his book *Ghosts and How to See Them*, he cites a scientific experiment in which a researcher held the blunt end of a pencil to the back of a woman. "[He] told her it was a lighted cigarette. Unconsciously, the mind of the subject reacted to the idea that it was indeed a lighted cigarette that had touched her back, and a 'burn' resulted."[42]

Not Such a Great Leap

Other researchers believe that it is not such a great leap from controlling the body in that way to controlling other matter. Modern poltergeist research is focusing on the possible relationship of RSPK to brain irregularities in poltergeist agents.

For example, a 1999 study examined a large number of young people thought to be agents of poltergeist activity. More than 4 percent of those had epilepsy, a medical disorder caused by abnormal electrical discharges in the brain. That is more than eight times the rate of epilepsy in the general population. Many researchers wonder if epilepsy or related brain irregularities could make RSPK more likely.

No one knows yet if RSPK is somehow connected to poltergeist activity, but it seems a promising lead. Julius, the Indiana man who is convinced that poltergeists were bouncing Ping-Pong balls in his home, says he hopes new information will provide answers. "It's easy for people to dismiss things like poltergeists and other paranormal events," he says. "It's all a big joke—easy to laugh at people who talk about [things like poltergeists]. I was the same way, I guess—I wouldn't have taken it seriously. But when it happens to you, it's all different. Then you hope scientists or whatever can find out more about this stuff, more solid information that can explain it all."[43]

CHAPTER 4

Investigating Ghosts

While countless frightening stories about ghosts exist, not much in the way of scientific proof has been found. The lack of hard evidence is a roadblock for people who would like to believe such stories.

"Everybody Knows Somebody Whose Brother Saw This Ghost"

Tom Guillen is a New York research chemist. He says he has heard many ghost stories, and part of him would love to believe that spirits and ghosts exist. However, he says, the stories seem more like drama than science.

"It's all so anecdotal," he says.

I think the stories are great and all the movies that are based on the stories. And around a campfire at night? Nothing better. But it's all based on different people's versions of their experiences, or someone else's experiences. Everybody knows somebody whose brother saw this ghost, and the brother is really honest and would never make up a story like that.

And all the people telling the stories say that there were 10 eyewitnesses who saw the ghost, and none of them would ever lie, either. But the fact is, some of these people I've heard tell these stories are really kind of hard to put faith in. They talk about ghosts causing power outages in the house, or how their cats are all traumatized by the ghosts, and it goes on and on. I'm a scientist. I deal in the kind of details that can be measured or counted. But this isn't like that. There isn't any solid evidence. [44]

"The Nature of the Beast"

Guillen says that the idea of "believing"—so crucial to paranormal research—should not matter if something is true. "Scientists don't believe or disbelieve in gravity," he says. "They don't believe or disbelieve that molecules exist. You don't need to believe in scientific fact. But if you ask somebody about ghosts, people talk about how you have to take these things on faith. I don't think you can expect to be taken seriously as science if belief is a key part of your field."[45]

Many ghost researchers would agree with Guillen's assessment. Their research is not clinical. Alex Felix, a former police officer and now a Chicago ghost investigator says his type of research is unlike chemistry and other sciences. "Because it's not an exact science, it's left open to criticism from non-believers," Felix says. "But that's the nature of the beast."[46]

Even so, they say, until they have the tools or technology sophisticated enough to prove that ghosts exist, they need to gather as much data as they can—however they can. And while ghost researchers do use a large number of instruments in their work, they frequently rely on a thorough interview with eyewitnesses as a starting point for each investigation.

"Better than the Average Person"

Many ghost researchers understand that some witnesses are more valuable than others. In his book *Poltergeists* Michael Clarkson says that he tended to pay close attention when police talked about such cases: "Generally, police tend to be solid witnesses, trained and experienced in knowing how to focus when something is happening quickly. As believable witnesses for so-called paranormal events, they should be better than the average person because they tend to be skeptical and sometimes cynical about potential trickery."[47]

Clarkson cites the case of 11-year-old John Mulvey of Ontario. The boy's parents had consulted with city engineers and building inspectors, hoping to find a natural cause for the levitation of furniture and other objects in their home, but with no success. They finally called police, who witnessed firsthand chairs and beds flipping over by themselves. Though they could not explain what was happening around the boy, they could provide researchers with their testimony.

"It was one of the scariest things I've ever been involved with," said Harry Fox, one of the officers. "At least in your normal work, if you're confronted with a big man, you can defend yourself. But this was different, unpredictable. I think it was some sort of invisible energy."[48]

Eliminating the Not-So-Ghostly

When investigating reports of ghostly activity, researchers try to eliminate other, more likely causes. "When we witness something that is new to us, or that we can't explain, we will do everything we can to determine if it has a natural explanation," says Rene Kruse, an industrial engineer who researches ghosts in her spare time. "We do, in fact, try to disprove almost every anomaly that we record. This way, what we are left with is more reliable." [49]

"They talk about ghosts causing power outages in the house, or how their cats are all traumatized by the ghosts, and it goes on and on. I'm a scientist. I deal in the kind of details that can be measured or counted. But this isn't like that. There isn't any solid evidence."

—A research chemist discussing the lack of scientific evidence of the existence of ghosts.

Often, what homeowners hear may be a combination of old plumbing and the normal creaking of an older house—and maybe a mouse or two inside the walls. Going into an investigation with a healthy respect for the paranormal is fine, say experts, but it is important to be realistic. "Not everything that goes bump in the night is a ghost," agrees Dave Schrader, a Minnesota ghost researcher. "Sometimes it's just the pipes knocking."[50]

In many cases the natural explanation can be disappointing to researchers who are convinced they have discovered something exciting. In one suspected poltergeist case in a New York apartment, heavy statues on a fireplace mantel moved by themselves. Though the phenomenon was exciting, the cause was far more mundane than a poltergeist. It turned out that the family in the apartment just below had a malfunctioning washing machine, and the vibrations were causing the statues to move.

A Shooting Light

An easy explanation was discovered for an odd event in a house that was once part of the Underground Railroad. The Underground Railroad was a route of houses owned by people who opposed slavery. They provided hiding places for slaves making their way to freedom in the North. Researchers have heard about many possible paranormal events in such houses. They say this is not surprising, for ghosts frequent places where people have felt intense emotions like fear and anger. This particular house was very old—built in the late 1700s. Like most others on that route, it had a secret room in its basement, where escaped slaves could hide as they made their perilous northward journey.

Investigators set up a video camera on a tripod in the room and turned it on. Then they left for several hours. When the investigators returned, they watched the tape to see if anything had occurred while they were gone. They were rewarded with an unusual sight. Several times, a bright light formed on the wall, just to the right of the camera, and then suddenly shot across the room.

The room had been closed and no source of light could have caused the phenomenon. It was perplexing, says one of the researchers. "We had never seen this phenomenon before," she recalls, "but we were very excited at the prospect of discovering something new." They returned to the house and set up the camera again to see if they could capture the shooting light a second time. They did, but the results were less exciting than they had hoped. "We eventually found that there was a small hole in the baseboard of a room upstairs. . . . When someone swept the baseboard of the wall above and the light hit the small hole, it shot light through the [underground] room, which had an amplified effect on the . . . camera. We had explained the cause of our mysterious shooting light."[51]

Fake Ghosts

Sometimes the suspected ghost turns out to be a fake. In some cases, what at first appeared to be a poltergeist turned out to be the creation by an imaginative—and needy—young person. Researchers say that in many of these cases the young persons desperately want adult attention. They enjoy being the center of attention as their parents, police, ghost researchers, and others try to find an explanation for the strange goings-on.

In other cases the motive is simply to make money. A resident ghost is a way for an inn or bed and breakfast to make money, and many create a ghost to do just that. Irene Meaney, a Connecticut restaurant manager, knows of more than a dozen inns throughout the area that boast of being haunted.

"There are probably many more that I don't know about," Meaney says.

> I think for some customers it makes staying there more interesting. It's a draw. Guests are assured the ghosts are just playful, you know. They don't do anything dangerous. Just causing lights to flicker or walls to knock once in a while.
>
> I've stayed in a Vermont [bed and breakfast]

where sometimes late at night one could hear a ghost softly singing opera. I'm sure the owners have something rigged up, a sound system or something. Then the next morning at breakfast, people compare notes on what they heard or saw. Is it real? I'd guess not, but I don't know. Either way, I think people enjoy thinking that they might have come in contact with a spirit of some kind. It's kind of exciting. [52]

The Most Devious Hoax

The most devious hoax of ghost activity as a way of making money occurred in Amityville, New York. It was there on November 13, 1974, that 23-year-old Ronald De Feo Jr. murdered his parents and four siblings at the family home, a large three-story house at 112 Ocean Avenue. A year later a young couple named George and Kathy Lutz bought the house, thrilled with the low asking price. Even when they were told about the house's violent history, they were not concerned. They did not believe in ghosts, they insisted, and moved into the house on December 18, 1975.

But less than a month after moving in the Lutzes moved out, leaving their furniture and other possessions behind. They reported that there had been ghosts, and that the spirits were aggressive and very frightening. They told about hooded ghosts, loud knocking in walls, and green slime oozing from the ceiling. They had been attacked by black flies in one of their children's rooms and had seen objects levitating.

The following year the Lutzes collaborated with writer Jay Anson on a book. Called *The Amityville Horror*, it was a best seller

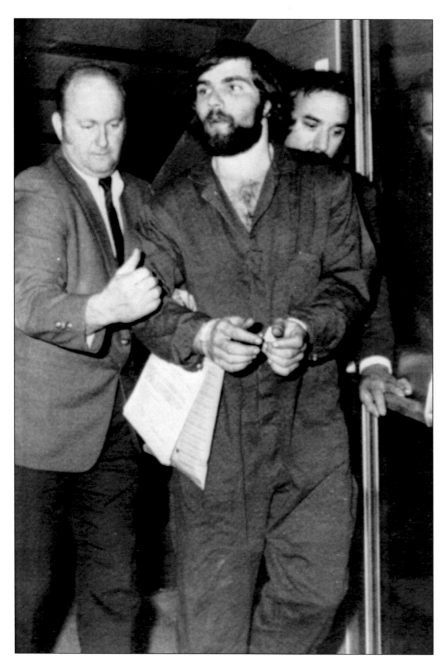

On November 13, 1974, 23-year-old Ronald De Feo Jr. (in hand-cuffs) murdered his parents and four siblings at the family home in Amityville, NY. A year later a young couple named George and Kathy Lutz bought the house but less than a month after moving in the Lutzes abruptly moved out, leaving their furniture and other possessions behind.

Jumping to Conclusions

Sometimes researchers can be fooled by their own findings. One inexperienced Massachusetts researcher demonstrated what he believed was photographic proof of a ghost. Part of the photo that included a window in the background showed an orange glow, which had not been visible to the photographer taking the picture. However, it turned out that the window was coated with plastic. What appeared to be an apparition was really a result of the camera's flash reflecting off the plastic.

and was soon made into a movie. Everyone, it seemed, was fascinated by the horrible paranormal events in the Amityville house. But it turned out that the whole story was a hoax. The Lutzes had invented the story about ghosts in the house. There had been no green slime or flies or levitating objects. It had all been a way for all involved to make a lot of money by writing a best-selling book about their fictitious experiences.

The Tools of the Trade

Ghost researchers take their work seriously even if others do not. They use a variety of tools to determine the nature of a ghost sighting and whether it is the result of paranormal activity.

One of the most basic of these tools is a camera. For more than a century people have tried to capture ghosts on film. While many photographs can be explained as frauds or dismissed as inconclusive, a few have continued to perplex ghost researchers. A 1959 photograph taken by a woman named Mabel Chinnery is one of the most famous. After she and her husband went to the cemetery to visit her mother's grave, Chinnery took a photograph of her husband in the front seat of their car. When the photo was developed it showed the image of her deceased mother in the back seat. Hundreds of experts have examined the photograph, and none have found any evidence of double exposure or reflections that could have caused such an image. One photograph expert declared, "I stake my reputation on the fact that the picture is genuine."[53]

"It's Kind of Like Christmas"

Ghost researchers today say that much of the photographic evidence is "found"—meaning that, as in the case of Chinnery's photo, a ghost's presence is not discovered until after the photos are examined. They say that in many cases researchers, who take hundreds of photos in an area where people have reported ghost activity, are later surprised at what the camera has captured.

While investigating a small hotel in Madera County, California, photographer Terry Campbell took two digital photographs in quick succession outside. The first showed a pear tree. The second, taken less than a second later, showed strands of a whitish mist near the top of the tree. While it was certainly not proof of a ghost, it was interesting to other researchers.

Campbell had not seen the mist when he took the picture, and that, he says, is the mystery that makes photography such an interesting tool in ghost research. "It's kind of like Christmas," he says. "You open up the presents and see what you got."[54]

"We Thought the Photo Was Brilliant"

Sometimes the eeriest surprises occur when no paranormal activity is even suspected. At a 2007 wedding at a castle in Scotland, what appears to be a ghost was captured on camera in one of the routine wedding photos. Best man Stuart White took many pictures at the reception, but in one, a strange form dressed in green can be seen floating near the wedding guests. White insisted later that he saw no such form when he took the picture: "I was taking photographs all day and this was just a quick snap of my wife and some friends. None of us noticed anything unusual at the time. It was only when I downloaded the images onto my computer after the wedding that we stumbled across this. It's incredible—we've looked at it over and over again and nobody can explain it."[55]

Far from being uneasy or frightened at the idea of a ghost at her wedding, the bride took the odd photograph in stride. "We thought the photo was brilliant," she says, "and we're quite honored we had an extra guest at our wedding—whoever it was."[56]

Tape Recordings

Ghost researchers rely on tape recorders as much as cameras. They often leave a tape recorder running while investigating a site that is believed to have ghost activity. Afterward when researchers play the tape, they occasionally hear voices—even though such voices could not be heard at the time. Two researchers from New England Paranormal Investigations had that experience while they were talking in one of the rooms of a house believed to be haunted. One researcher addressed the room by asking, "Are you angry that people are here?"[57] They heard no answer until later when they replayed the tape. After the question was asked there was silence, and then the hiss of the tape recorder grew louder. A very clear, hoarse whisper answered, "We're angry."[58]

Researcher Sherri Higgins had a similar experience. She and a coworker were walking through a local cemetery. She made a comment about how beautiful and peaceful the old cemetery was. "Later," Higgins recalls, "when we listened to the recording, after I said, 'What a peaceful area,' an eerie whisper of a clearly female voice said, 'Peaceful.' We almost fell over, and the goosebumps rose on our arms. We played that tape over about twenty times."[59]

Electromagnetic Fields

Some tools are useful to researchers, but they are not sure why. One is an Electromagnetic Frequency (EMF) meter, an instrument that measures the amount of electromagnetism in an area. For many years ghost researchers have noticed that in places believed to be haunted, the amount of electromagnetism is very high. EMF is measured in units called milligauss (mG). A normal reading is between 1 and 2 mG, but in supposedly haunted places it can spike to 100 mG or more. Researcher Loyd Auerbach believes there is something in the high levels of electromagnetism that allows ghosts to be seen.

"Somehow, every once in a while, the unusual magnetic energy allows living people to see something that has happened at that location sometime in the past."

—A researcher discussing the link between electromagnetism and ghosts.

Did You Know?

According to ghost researchers unexplained extreme changes in temperature can be a sign of a ghostly presence.

We're not sure what causes this phenomenon, but it probably has something to do with the environment. Somehow, every once in a while, the unusual magnetic energy allows living people to see something that has happened at that location sometime in the past. The ghost someone sees in this situation is really an image from the past, not an actual ghost. I think the image someone sees is like a visual footprint left behind within the magnetic field that's present.[60]

Whatever the reason for the high EMF levels, many investigators try to keep track of the variations in frequency in areas in which they are working. Investigators take readings in a house twice—once with power in the house on, and once with everything turned off. That way they can eliminate appliances like refrigerators and ovens as a source of high EMFs.

Temperature Variations

Ghost researchers are also interested in unexplained dips in temperature. They monitor the temperature using a special sort of thermometer called a thermal scanner. Shaped a little like a gun, an investigator simply aims it at a part of the room and pulls the trigger for an instant reading. This can show a very small area that is cold; sometimes a cold spot signifies the presence of a ghost.

Extreme temperature change can also be a sign of a ghostly presence. Ghost investigator Linda Zimmermann was working with an associate in the parlor of a house in which a lot of paranormal activity had been reported. She recalls that the temperature went from comfortable to icy cold very quickly: "As Bob and I stood in the center of the room . . . a deathly chill passed through us going from right to left. The temperature seemed to drop by at least forty degrees and at that moment the EMF meter spiked to its highest reading. The icy air persisted for 10 to 15 seconds, and the moment it passed, the meter returned to zero."[61]

A Fool's Errand?

While every ghost researcher wants to find proof that ghosts are real, most realize the limitations of their work. Ghost researcher Troy Taylor says absolute proof is hard to come by. "We can provide evidence or circumstantial proof of it," he says, "but we can't ultimately prove that ghosts exist. . . . I have not yet seen evidence, beyond a reasonable doubt, that ghosts exist. I have seen a lot of great circumstantial evidence, but that's all it is."[62]

Skeptics such as Joe Nickell question whether the pairing of science and ghost investigations is even possible. Even to entertain the notion of ghosts and spirits is an admission by researchers that such things are possible, he says. "These people have to come to terms with the fact," says Nickell, "that when someone dies, brain activity ceases. Science has never confirmed a single ghost. This [ghost research] is a fool's errand."[63]

Even so, the researchers do not give up. "Einstein said energy cannot be created or destroyed," says researcher Joe Ward. "So when we die, our energy is still there."[64] Like Ward, many researchers believe the important thing is to keep an open mind.

CHAPTER 5

Should They Stay or Should They Go?

O nce a ghost investigator has discovered strong proof that ghosts may be present in a location, the owner must decide on the next step. In many cases the owners simply move, choosing not to remain in a haunted place. For some, however, the idea of living alongside ghosts is not completely out of the question. In fact, a surprising number of people have actually chosen to coexist with spirits.

Cursed

One of the most famous examples of someone choosing to live with ghosts is Sarah Winchester. In the late 1800s she was married to William Winchester, whose father had invented the repeating rifle, a vast improvement over the slow, muzzle-loading guns of the time. The Winchester repeating rifles, sold to the Union army in the Civil War, were credited with helping the

North win that war. Not surprisingly, the Winchester Repeating Rifle Company made the family very wealthy.

Though she seemed to be on the brink of a happy life, young Sarah Winchester's world soon fell apart. Her baby daughter sickened and died when she was only nine days old. Out of her mind with grief, Sarah Winchester withdrew into her own thoughts. Just as she began to come to grips with her loss, her husband died of tuberculosis.

Needing a way to go on with her shattered life, she consulted a spiritualist, a woman who was reputed to be able to contact the spirit world. The woman told Winchester that her husband had a message for her. He said that there was a curse on the Winchesters because of the thousands of people who had been killed by the repeating rifle. The curse had killed their baby, and it had killed him, too.

The spiritualist conveyed the husband's words to Winchester. He warned that she was in danger and that she must follow his instructions. "You must start a new life and build a home for yourself and for the spirits who have fallen from this terrible weapon. . . . You can never stop building the house. If you continue building, you will live. Stop, and you will die."[65]

Twenty-Four-Hour Construction

Winchester sold her home and headed to California, where she found a small, 6-room farmhouse on 162 acres of land in the Santa Clara Valley. She promptly hired 22 carpenters, so that there would be at least one crew working 24 hours a day, 7 days a week. She began creating plans for dozens of new rooms for the ghosts.

But while she built the house for the ghosts, she was terrified

The Winchester house has 160 rooms. Sarah Winchester was told if she stopped building additions onto the house spirits of those killed by rifles made by the Winchester Repeating Rifle Company would kill her.

that they would find her. To keep them at bay, her designs were a dizzying labyrinth of stairways that went to the ceiling, rooms inside of rooms, windows on the floor, and doors that opened to a 3-story drop to the lawn below.

Over the next 37 years she continued to build. Her construction crews used so much lumber and her rooms required so many furnishings that a railroad track was laid from the main line nearby to her property. Though Winchester was beyond wealthy from her inheritance (she owned 49 percent of the rifle company, valued at $20 million in 1884), she used most of it on her ever-expanding home. By the time she died there in 1922 the Winchester house had more than 160 rooms—plenty of room for ghosts and for the woman who wished to avoid them.

Imaginary Friends

But not every person who coexists with a ghost does so with the fear that Winchester had.

In fact, many ghost researchers believe that at any given time, tens of thousands of children are living quite happily with ghosts—and their parents are not even aware of it. These researchers suggest that in many cases, what are termed "imaginary playmates" by parents are actually child ghosts who have befriended living children.

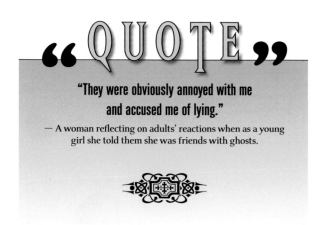

"They were obviously annoyed with me and accused me of lying."

— A woman reflecting on adults' reactions when as a young girl she told them she was friends with ghosts.

Eileen Garrett, who grew up to become a psychic, recalls the imaginary playmates she had as a little girl:

> There were two little girls and a boy. I believe that I first met them sometime before I went to school, at about four years old. I first saw them framed in the doorway; they stood, as children will, intent on looking. I joined them, and after that they came to see me daily. Sometimes they stayed all day, sometimes but a little while, but no day passed of which they were not a part.

Garrett says that the adults in her life never believed that her friends existed. "They were obviously annoyed with me," she says, "and accused me of lying. They ridiculed the whole idea of the existence of these playmates, yet I touched them, and found that they were soft and warm, even as I [was]."[66]

Open Minds

Many experts suggest that children are able to see ghosts more easily than adults because their minds are still open to possibilities. They have not yet learned that some things seem impossible. "Kids operate on a different plane than adults," agrees ghost researcher Grace Donne.

> They seem to take things as they seem. They don't try to force a situation into a preconceived idea about how things *should be.* On the other hand, we [adults] in such a situation, seeing a strange person materialize out of nowhere, call

that a hallucination. We'd be quick to mentally run down the things that could cause us to see something that wasn't there. Do we have a brain tumor? Do we have a high fever? Is there something wrong with our vision? But a child would just accept it.[67]

That seems to have been the case in Airth Castle in Stirlingshire, Scotland. Part of the castle burned down in the 1800s, but the rest was turned into a hotel. A nanny and two young children were killed in the blaze, and since then some visitors have heard a woman's voice frantically asking if anyone has seen the children. But it is some of the youngest visitors to the hotel who have been able to see the child ghosts. Hotel manager Hugh Loudon recalls one eerie occurrence. "I remember [a] family whose children said they weren't coming down to breakfast because they wanted to play with their two new friends. But there were no other children staying at the hotel." [68]

Making Peace with Ghosts

Some people have found a way to share space with ghostly residents and so have no need to go elsewhere. Bob Lurtsema, a former Minnesota Vikings football player, opened a restaurant in Burnsville, Minnesota, called Benchwarmer Bob's. Soon after the restaurant opened, some very strange events took place.

The late-night cleaning crew would stack chairs on top of tables, and soon two would be discovered back on the floor, facing each other as if two people were having a conversation. Elevators inexplicably began going up and down when no one was inside them. Lurtsema says he knew he had to do something, for his workers were becoming very frightened.

"On two separate occasions I have had American Indians come out and they explained things about burial grounds," he says. "They said if you make peace with them [the spirits] and put something up to show that you believe, they won't bother you anymore."[69]

Over the entrance to Benchwarmer Bob's, Lurtsema hung a dream catcher, a handmade Native American willow hoop strung with netting. Dream catchers are believed to be capable of sifting out bad dreams and spirits from good ones, and their power seemed to work for Lurtsema. Soon after placing the dream catcher in his restaurant, most of the ghostly activity stopped. Evidently, Lurtsema was able to find a way to share the space with the spirits of long-dead Native Americans some believe are buried beneath.

"We Don't Just Get This Gift for Ourselves"

But while in many cases the living choose to find a peaceful way to coexist with ghosts, it is far more common for people to want ghosts in their lives to go away. Donne says it is not a surprising reaction. "I'm always a little startled whenever a person is *not* eager to get rid of a ghost. Typically, the client feels relief in a sense that they were not imagining the [paranormal] activity, and once that relief passes, the next question is 'Now, what do we do?'" Donne, like most ghost researchers, is not capable of removing ghosts from premises, but she assures clients that there are people who are. "I have names of psychics that I can give clients," she says.

Bob Lurtsema, left, a former NFL player, opened a restaurant in Minnesota apparently on an old Native American burial ground. When strange things began to happen, he put up a dream catcher and most of the activity stopped.

"I'm always a little startled whenever a person is *not* eager to get rid of a ghost."

—A ghost researcher discussing surprising reactions people have when told they have a ghost in their home.

They can do one of two things—because they can sense the presence of ghosts, they can verify what our instruments show. You have to remember that just because I get a [thermal] scanner reading that shows a big dip in temperature in one area of a room, that isn't proof that there is a ghost there. But a psychic can come in and verify that yes, that's exactly what it is. He or she has that gift.[70]

Jean Kellet, a Minnesota psychic, strongly believes that ghosts do not belong in the living world and that a pyschic's ability should be used to help them move on. She says it is the welfare of the ghosts that she is concerned with primarily. "My feeling is, if there is some way to help them and let them know there is some peace [somewhere else]," Kellet explains, "then we should be doing that. We don't get this gift just for ourselves and our own gain."[71]

"Lighter than a Feather"

Psychics who deal with haunted spaces talk about "seeing" spirits, but it is a different kind of sight than what most people have. Echo Bodine, a psychic who has had great success in helping ghosts move along to the spirit world, admits that her gift is difficult to explain, but it has to do with the difference in the sort of energy given out by living people and ghosts.

"We humans have a dense energy," she says. "We're heavy. Our vibration or energy is heavy. A soul or spirit is lighter than a feather. In order to connect with them, we have to raise our energy level to that very light vibration, and that can be very draining physically."[72]

When a psychic enters a house or other building, he or she can usually sense very quickly that spirit energy is there. Bodine says that she rarely senses ghosts when she is not working. However, once in a while she will be in such a relaxed, open state of mind that ghosts will be visible to her. On one occasion, she and her fiancé had gone out of town. She walked into the sitting room of an inn to read about restaurants in the area, she remembers, "and there, sitting about a foot above the couch, was the spirit of a young man. He looked up at me and I smiled at him, which startled him. He told me he had died in Vietnam and that this was his hometown. Seemed like a nice enough fellow, and after reminding myself that I was there to relax, not work, I left the room and went back to ours." [73]

Haunting Three Rooms

As mentioned earlier, spirits have a variety of reasons for remaining on Earth, and psychics say they can usually find out very quickly what a particular spirit's reason is. In many cases the motivation is deep love for living relatives or friends. However, most psychics say the motive for remaining earthbound makes no difference. No matter how loving the emotions, all of a ghost's attempts to contact or send messages to its loved ones are frightening to them, not reassuring.

Psychic Carol Lowell tells of a situation in which a family was experiencing odd occurrences. Appliances would turn on and off by themselves, and there was a smell of smoke which seemed to have no source. The desperate homeowner said that his family was very nervous, and he wanted a psychic to come and make sense of the situation.

Lowell did a walk-through of the home and believed that the spirit was that of an older man. She felt his energy in 3 rooms—the master bedroom, the son's room, and the living room. "In these 3 rooms," says Lowell, "his energy was the strongest. When the couple would go to bed, he would go down to the son's room, and when the son would be in his room, he would retreat to the living room."[74]

Lowell was able to see the spirit, and he spoke to her. As it turned out, he was the father of her client, and he had been trying hard to get his son's attention, to let him know that he was there. "He showed me his heart," recalls Lowell. "I thought he was trying to tell me that he had died of a heart attack, but that was not the case. He had tears in his eyes and said that when he died it broke his heart to leave his family. He loved them so much that he didn't want to go, so he never crossed over."[75]

She was able to use her psychic abilities to communicate with him. She convinced him he would be much happier—and his family much less stressed—if he moved on into the spirit world. He finally agreed, and the situation was resolved.

Multiple Problems

In many cases where psychics are brought in to remove a ghost from a home or other building, they realize that there is more than one spirit doing the haunting. That was the case in Mark Houser's home. Echo Bodine was the psychic who offered to help, and it took very little time for her to see that there were eight ghosts residing in Houser's home. And they all had their own reasons for remaining on Earth.

Houser and his two children had been well aware of the child ghosts, for Houser's son had seen them—and they all had heard the children's voices and the sound of their ball bouncing on the floor upstairs. Bodine explains that she sat on the floor so she

An Ancient Exorcism

In Bon, a religion that was practiced in India and Tibet centuries before Buddhism, exorcisms took place on a regular basis—and are still practiced in some parts of Asia today. The priest, or lama, meditates about the ghost or demon that is haunting a place or person. Once he has an image of the ghost, he creates a figure out of flour and butter. After it is dry, he stabs it, symbolically killing the ghost. The figure is then cut into pieces, which are burned. The ashes are buried, and a small tower of rocks is erected over the site. From that day on, that site is considered powerful and very dangerous ground.

would be at their level, found out their names, and was not surprised to get responses very typical of young children:

> Annie [one of the spirits] said they all lived in a
> house over there, and they pointed in a direction

west of the house. I asked her if they were related to each other, and she said no, that they were not related, but had all lived together, gotten sick and died around the same time. I asked her why they didn't go to the other side, and she said they didn't want to, they just wanted to play. [76]

Bodine told Houser what the children had said, and he told her that he had learned from neighbors that there used to be an orphanage in the neighborhood many years ago and that it had burned down. Bodine told the children that it was important for them to go, and that they would have fun on the other side, too. She convinced one of the older children, a boy named Dougy, to lead them.

One Mean, One Confused

Those six ghosts were easy to talk with, but Bodine had a more difficult time with the other two. One was an elderly man she found downstairs in the basement. His name was Elmer, he said, but he seemed confused about almost everything else. Like many ghosts, Elmer did not realize that he was dead and had been hanging around the basement, wondering where his wife, Rose, was.

Bodine says that she used spirits guides—helpful ghosts she had met in other circumstances—that were willing to assist her in tough cases. They got Rose from the other side and got Elmer to go with her. "It was one of those sweet reunions," recalls Bodine, "where all it took was getting them back together to get the stuck one to move to the other side."[77]

The other ghost was a young man named Roger. He was something of a bully, saying he enjoyed scaring the ghost children in the attic. He lived in the house because he had not been able to afford a nice house when he was alive, he told Bodine. He did not want to go to the other side, for he was worried that he would not be able to date women there—a high priority for him.

Bodine knew that it was important to be firm with Roger, and that as the owner of the house, Houser should be the one to insist that Roger leave. While Bodine assured Roger that he would most certainly be able to meet women in the spirit world, Houser very forcefully told Roger that he had no business remaining in the house. It was time to leave. Eventually he moved on. All eight of the troublesome ghosts were gone.

Exorcism: A Casting Out

Sometimes talk does not succeed in getting ghosts to move on. Some people have turned to a centuries-old ritual known as exorcism. The term *exorcism* means "a casting out." And while the work many psychics do can cast out spirits, the term most often refers to a specific religious rite.

In the sixteenth century the Roman Catholic Church created a rite of exorcism for casting out demons. For centuries the exorcism cases involved what the church called "possession"—a situation in which a demon invaded the body of a living person. Only certain priests could perform an exorcism, and the specifics of the Latin language ceremony were kept secret. In 2000 the Vatican made the decision to allow more priests to learn the rite of exorcism, and because it was believed that evil was on the upswing in the modern world, they added house exorcisms to the ceremony.

Pastor Hugo Alvarez is one of Mexico's foremost exorcists, handling a dozen or more cases in Mexico City each week. Before each one, he goes through a very strict regimen of fasting and prayer to prepare himself for what the church considers a conflict between good and evil. "It's a beautiful rite," he says, "a very solemn and serious celebration."[78]

Not Just a Catholic Rite

Religious exorcisms are not limited to the Catholic Church. Leaders of the Anglican Church of England, for example, agree that the demand for exorcisms of haunted places has grown in recent years. Using prayers and holy water taken from the baptismal font, Anglican priests perform blessings on houses troubled with unexplained activity.

Some ghost researchers, however, feel that there are drawbacks to religious exorcisms. "The problem with priests is that most of them are not psychic," says Paul, a spokesman for London's Spirit Rescue Service—self-proclaimed "ghostbusters" who use a combination of psychic techniques and ceremony in their work. "They can't communicate with the ghosts and so they just sprinkle holy water over the walls and tell [the ghost] to be gone. The ghost is unsettled and moves on somewhere else without being saved."[79]

The Spirit Rescue Service believes that their first responsibility is to the unsettled spirit. They try to psychically communicate with the spirit, as well as using some of the most ancient ceremonial tools of ghost removal, such meditation and burning sage—a fragrance believed to be unpleasant to spirits.

Maybe in the Future

But while millions of people say they believe in the existence of ghosts, those who deal with the spirit world are often met with a lot of skepticism, if not downright ridicule. However, ghost re-

The term exorcism means "a casting out." And while the work many psychics do can cast out spirits, the term most often refers to a specific religious rite. Priests in Italy listen to a lesson on exorcism while studying the book Ritual of Exorcisms and Prayers for Particular Circumstances.

searchers are determined to carry on their work, as are psychics, exorcists, and others who deal in the study of ghosts or the removal of earthbound spirits.

Though the existence of ghosts has not been proved to the satisfaction of scientists, some researchers are confident that it will happen. After all, one of the most brilliant scientists in history, Albert Einstein, once commented on the danger of dismissing what cannot be proved. "It is possible," he said, "that there exist emanations that are still unknown to us. Do you remember how electrical currents and unseen waves were laughed at?"[80] Perhaps ghosts are an example of one of these emanations, and their existence will be validated in the future.

NOTES

Introduction: The Ghosts in the Attic

1. Quoted in Peg Meier, "Ghost Story," *Minneapolis Star Tribune*, May 17, 1996, p. 1B.
2. Mark Houser, telephone interview with author, June 3, 2007.
3. Houser, telephone interview.
4. Houser, telephone interview.
5. Houser, telephone interview.
6. Quoted in Meier, "Ghost Story," p. 1B.
7. Julius, telephone interview with author, July 15, 2007.

Chapter 1: A World of Spirits

8. Quoted in Tom Ogden, *The Complete Idiot's Guide to Ghosts and Hauntings.* New York: Alpha, 2004, p. 19.
9. Quoted in Rosemary Ellen Gulley, *The Encyclopedia of Ghosts and Spirits.* New York: Facts On File, 2000, p. 23.
10. Quoted in Jason Rich, *Everything Ghost Book: Spooky Stories of Haunted Houses, Phantom Spirits, Unexplained Mysteries, and More.* Avon, MA: Adams Media, 2001, p. 8.
11. Quoted in Bob Rowland, "Weeks After Girl's Slaying, Mysterious Image Appears," *San Diego Union*, July 18, 1991, p. A1.
12. Quoted in Rowland, "Weeks After Girl's Slaying," p. A1.
13. Quoted in Rowland, "Weeks After Girl's Slaying," p. A1.
14. Ogden, *The Complete Idiot's Guide to Ghosts and Hauntings*, p. 47.
15. Quoted in Winter Steel, "Doubles: Doppelgangers." www.wintersteel.com.
16. Quoted in Joanne Austin, *Weird Hauntings: True Tales of Ghostly Places.* New York: Sterling, 2006, p. 100.
17. Quoted in The Astral World, "Echoes of Dieppe." www.theastralworld.com.

Chapter 2: Why Spirits Remain

18. Grace Donne, interview with author, Alexandria, Minnesota, June 14, 2007.
19. Quoted in John Burdett, "Thais Have Their Own Response to Tragedy," *Minneapolis Star Tribune*, January 18, 2005.
20. Quoted in Burdett, "Thais Have Their Own Response."
21. Jen Olafson, interview with author, Minneapolis, Minnesota, July 3, 2007.
22. Olafson, interview.
23. Olafson, interview.
24. Quoted in Linda Zimmermann, *Ghost Investigator: Haunting of the Hudson Valley.* Blooming Grove, NY: Spirited, 2002, p. 152.

25. Quoted in Sherry Steiger, *Face to Face with the Unknown: True Stories About Young People's Encounters with the Unexplained.* New York: Tor, 2001, p. 29.

26. Quoted in John G. Fuller, *The Ghost of Flight 401.* New York: Berkley, 1976, p. 4.

27. Quoted in Fuller, *The Ghost of Flight 401*, p. 129.

28. Quoted in Fuller, *The Ghost of Flight 401*, p. xi.

29. Quoted in Weird and Haunted Chicago, "Mary—The Elusive Ghost." www.prairie ghosts. com.

30. Quoted in *Weird and Haunted Chicago*, "Mary—The Elusive Ghost."

Chapter 3: Poltergeists

31. Peter Underwood, *Ghosts and How to See Them.* London: Anaya, 1993, p.31.

32. Julius, telephone interview.

33. Quoted in Chris Laursen, "Rock the House," Sue Darroch and Matthew Didier's Paranormal Blog, June 20, 2007. http://seminars.torontoghosts.org.

34. Quoted in Laurson, "Rock the House."

35. David Kahn, "A Home's Bad Vibration," *Newsday Online.* www.newsday.com.

36. Troy Taylor, "Poltergeists," *Ghosts of the Prairie.* www.prairieghosts.com.

37. Quoted in Michael Clarkson, *Poltergeists: Examining Mysteries of the Paranormal.* Buffalo, NY: Firefly, 2005, p. 21.

38. Quoted in Editors of Time-Life, *Hauntings.* Alexandria, VA: Time-Life, 1989, pp. 72–73.

39. Quoted in Clarkson, *Poltergeists*, p. 22.

40. Quoted in Clarkson, *Poltergeists*, p. 184.

41. Paul Johnson, interview with author, Minneapolis, Minnesota, June 29, 2007.

42. Underwood, *Ghosts and How to See Them*, p. 32.

43. Julius, interview.

Chapter 4: Investigating Ghosts

44. Tom Guillen, telephone interview with author, July 13, 2007.

45. Guillen, telephone interview.

46. Quoted in Gerry Smith, "Hunting Midwest Haunts," *Chicago Tribune*, June 20, 2007, p. 2NW.

47. Clarkson, *Poltergeists*, p. 10.

48. Quoted in Clarkson, *Poltergeists*, pp. 59–60.

49. Quoted in J. Michael Krivyanski, "Probing the Phenomena Called Ghosts," *World & I*, August 2001, p. 140.

50. Quoted in Chris Welsch, "Pair of Normal Guys Run Paranormal Tours," *Minneapolis Star Tribune*, March 25, 2007, p. 1 A.

51. Quoted in Krivyanski, "Probing the Phenomena Called Ghosts," p. 140.

52. Irene Meaney, telephone interview with author, July 11, 2007.

53. Quoted in Editors of Time-Life, *Hauntings*, p. 26.

54. Quoted in Felicia Cousart Matlosz, "G-g-g-ghosts!" *Fresno (CA) Bee*, March 20, 2007, p. E1.

55. Quoted in Steve Smith, "Wedding Ghost," *London Daily Mirror*, April 1, 2007, p. 20.

56. Quoted in Smith, "Wedding Ghost," p. 20.

57. Quoted in Jennifer Huberdeau, "Ghost Hunting in Houghton Mansion," *North Adams (MA) Transcript*, April 1, 2007.

58. Quoted in Huberdeau, "Ghost Hunting in Houghton Mansion."

59. Quoted in Krivyanski, "Probing the Phenomena Called Ghosts," p. 140.

60. Quoted in Rich, *The Everything Ghost Book*, p. 26.

61. Zimmermann, *Ghost Investigator*, p. 65.

62. Quoted in Smith, "Hunting Midwest Haunts," p. 2NW.

63. Quoted in Rich, *The Everything Ghost Book*, p. 70.

64. Quoted in Christian Boone, "Ghost Luster Lost," *Atlanta Journal-Constitution*, January 22, 2007, p. B1.

Chapter 5: Should They Stay or Should They Go?

65. Quoted in Troy Taylor, "The Winchester Mystery House." www.prairieghosts.com.

66. Quoted in Hilary Evans and Patrick Huyghe, *The Field Guide to Ghosts and Other Apparitions*. New York: Quill, 2000, pp, 14–15.

67. Donne, interview.

68. Quoted in Smith, "Wedding Ghost," p. 20.

69. Quoted in Gina Teel, *Ghost Stories of Minnesota*. Edmonton, AB: Ghost House, 2001, p. 84.

70. Donne, interview.

71. Quoted in Teel, *Ghost Stories of Minnesota*, p. 154.

72. Echo Bodine, *Relax, It's Only a Ghost: My Adventures with Spirits, Hauntings, and Things That Go Bump in the Night*. Boston: Element, 2000, p. xv.

73. Bodine, *Relax, It's Only a Ghost*, p. xix.

74. Quoted in Teel, *Ghost Stories of Minnesota*, p. 170.

75. Quoted in Teel, *Ghost Stories of Minnesota*, p. 171.

76. Bodine, *Relax, It's Only a Ghost*, p. 70.

77. Bodine, *Relax, It's Only a Ghost*, p. 71.

78. Quoted in Jo Tuckman, "Exorcists in Demand to Expel Mexico's Demons," *Manchester Guardian*, February 15, 2001, p. 18.

79. Quoted in Mary Wakefield, "Exorcising Rites," *Spectator*, September 28, 2002, p. 56.

80. Quoted in Seek to Know, "Holistic Services." www.seek2know.net.

FOR FURTHER RESEARCH

Books

J. Allan Danelek, *The Case For Ghosts: An Objective Look at the Paranormal.* Woodbury, MN: Llewelyn, 2006. Very readable, with a good section on ghost research tools, as well as helpful information on various types of ghosts.

Joel Martin and William J. Birnes, *The Haunting of Presidents: A Paranormal History of the U.S. Presidency.* New York: Signet, 2003. An extensive bibliography, with good stories about presidents and their relationships to ghosts and spirits.

Michael Norman, *Haunted Homeland.* New York: Forge, 2006. Gives details on some of the most haunted houses in the United States and legends surrounding them. Very comprehensive bibliography.

Katherine Ramsland, *Ghost: A Firsthand Account into the World of Paranormal Activity.* New York: St. Martin's, 2001. Good information on spirit photography, and a helpful index.

William Roll and Valerie Storey, *Unleashed: Of Poltergeists and Murder: The Curious Story of Tina Resch.* New York: Paraview, 2002. Very thorough case study of the troubled teen, with a lot of good first-person observations.

Periodicals

W. Ritchie Benedict, "A Century of Ghosts and Hauntings," *Fate*, June 2004.

Lillian E. Hefferman, "It's No Image; Sign Showing Laura's Photo," *San Diego Tribune*, August 2, 1991.

Valerie Porter, "Kenny Kingston's Haunted Hollywood," *Fate*, December 2005.

Web Sites

American Folklore (www.americanfolklore.net/spooky-stories.html). This site features a top-10 list of the scariest ghost stories in American history, including the famous "Black Dog of Hanging Hills" tale.

American Society for Psychical Research (www.aspr.com). The ASPR investigates claims of paranormal events and has a number of links to information on ghosts, hauntings, and near-death experiences.

Ghost Research Society (www.ghost research.org). This group investigates ghosts using the most up-to-date technological tools. The Web site has a number of links including one to its most famous cases and another to a discussion of the equipment used by investigators.

Haunted Chicago (www.hauntedchicago.com). Lots of good information on ghosts and spirits that have been haunting the city for centuries. Includes photographs and eyewitness accounts, as well as good information about the tools used by ghost researchers.

International Ghost Hunters Society (www.ghostweb.com). This site has video clips, photos, and electronic voice phenomenon evidence, as well as a thorough recommended-reading list for people serious about researching ghostly phenomena.

INDEX

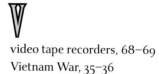

About the Author

Gail Stewart is the author of more than 220 books for children and teens. She loves baseball, especially the Minnesota Twins. She is also a fan of the Gustavus Adolphus Men's Soccer Team. She and her husband are the parents of three sons and live in Minneapolis, Minnesota.